Joash Woodrow

Joash Woodrow

Nicholas Usherwood and Christopher P. Wood

THE JOASH WOODROW COLLECTION
IN ASSOCIATION WITH 108 FINE ART

for Joash

First published in 2004 by
The Joash Woodrow Collection
in association with 108 Fine Art

108 Contemporary Fine Art
108 West End Avenue
Harrogate HG2 9BT
UK

© The Joash Woodrow Collection

All rights reserved. No part of this book may be
reprinted or reproduced or utilised in any form or
by any electronic, mechanical or other means,
now known or hereafter invented, including
photocopying and recording, or in any information
storage or retrieval system, without permission in
writing from the publisher.

ISBN 0 9547817 0 8

Designed by Philip Lewis
Photography by Glen Segal
Printed and bound in Great Britain by
B A S Printers Ltd, Salisbury

FRONT COVER *Gilbert Looking Down* (detail)
BACK COVER *Bearded Man on a White Horse with a Standing Figure* (detail)
FRONTISPIECE *Yellow Fence and Black Trees* (detail)
PAGE 6 *Blue Jug and Bowl of Yellow Fruit* (detail)
PAGE 8 *Portrait of a Man* (detail)
PAGES 44–45 *Portrait of a Man Wearing Glasses* (detail)
PAGES 76–77 *The Athlete* (detail)
PAGES 110–111 *Fragmented Table Top Still Life* (detail)
PAGES 144–145 *White Picket Fences* (detail)
PAGES 184–185 *Portrait of a Man and Woman* (detail)
PAGES 220–221 Drawing from one of 'The Magazine of Art' volumes (detail)

Contents

Acknowledgements 7

Chronology 9

Introduction 10
ANDREW STEWART

Coming in from afar:
The life and work of Joash Woodrow 18
NICHOLAS USHERWOOD AND CHRISTOPHER P. WOOD

A brother's story 36
SAUL WOODROW

Growing up with Joash 38
PAUL WOODROW

Plates

Portraits 44

Group studies 76

Animal and still life studies 110

Landscapes 144

Drawings, collage and sculpture 184

The Books 220

List of collectors 240

Acknowledgements

We would like to thank a growing number of individuals who have championed the work of Joash Woodrow since the re-discovery of the collection. Gillian Stewart, Tim Wood and Sarah Charneca who have devoted much of their time to the conservation and cataloguing of Joash's work. Nicholas Bradford who has volunteered on many occasions to help hang Joash Woodrow exhibitions at 108. Jilly Szaybo for her infectious enthusiasm and good nature. Professor Hugo Mascie Taylor, Paul Longstaff and Yvonne Wilson for their time and kind assistance in promoting the work of Joash and, to the following people who have supported the work of Joash Woodrow in their own ways: Mr Trevor Wilson, Selina Thorp, John Thorp, Tony Thompson, Ian and Lorraine Moore, Dan and Jacqui Simpson, Brian Dooks, Marilyn Smith and Steve Hoyle, Graeme Wood, Mr and Mrs Steven Smith, Peter Smith, Mr and Mrs John Spooner, Glen Segal, Jeanna and Dave Prior, Dr Richard Dobbins, Mr ands Mrs Hugh Dunn, Richard Aronowitz-Mercer, Mr Martin Ephson, Dennis Creffield, Cyril Satorsky, the late Colin Hayes, Alfred Daniels, Peter Doefler, Neil Holroyd, Nigel Walsh and Tim Wilcox. A special thank you to Scarlett and India Stewart for allowing their home to be used for the exhibition of works by Joash Woodrow.

Chronology

1927	Born Leeds, 7 April
1942–45	Student at Leeds College of Art
1945–48	National Service, as a cartographer, spent largely in Egypt
1948–50	Return to The Leeds College of Art to complete studies
1950–53	Scholarship to The Royal College of Art
1951	Death of his father, Harry (Herzl)
1953–56	Living and working in London (as an accountant)
1956	Return to the family home in Chapel Allerton, Leeds where he continued to live until 2000
1961	Death of his mother, Rebecca (Rifki)
2000	Left Chapel Allerton to live in sheltered accommodation in Manchester
2002	First solo exhibition at 108 Gallery, Harrogate
2003	Second solo exhibition at 108 Gallery, Harrogate
2004	Exhibition of his Leeds landscapes, Leeds City Art Gallery
2005	Major touring exhibition – opening venue, Manchester Art Gallery

Introduction

Andrew Stewart

During the past twenty years having worked as an artist, conservator, curator, auction house picture specialist, and most recently gallery owner I have on occasions experienced the thrill of discovering a forgotten or previously overlooked painting of great quality. Contemporary art too provides an enormous amount of satisfaction, working with stimulating, creative individuals. With time I am increasingly aware that we are constantly at a point where new, inspiring art may emerge at any moment, visible to all with hindsight, but often neglected in its own time. With this said I would like to remember that when I first glimpsed the work of Joash Woodrow I had no doubt as to the obvious qualities of his work; but this would be untrue.

My introduction to the work of Joash came through a visit to the painter Christopher Wood at his studio in Leeds in 2001. He had bought a leather bound Victorian 'Magazine of Art' from a bookshop in Harrogate. Inside the book an artist had drawn on the original illustrations and photographs, using these images of antiquity, architecture and reproductions of art works as the background for his own small paintings and drawings (pages 220 to 239). Christopher informed me that the book had been part of a collection of some several thousand, cleared from an artist's studio in Leeds. Although some were signed I was unfamiliar with the artist's work and was surprised not to find any reference to him in the standard textbooks. The following afternoon, together with my colleague Tim Wood, I visited the bookshop where I purchased the remaining six books. Looking at the drawings I could see that the artist had an inventive use of line and composition and had undoubtedly been trained through the art college system.

Later that day contact was made with Sylvia Woodrow who invited me to the house to see the work. My memories of the day are clear. A snowy, Sunday morning, I arrived at a post-war house in North Leeds where I was greeted by Saul and Sylvia Woodrow. Saul told me that Joash had lived alone in the house since the death of his brother Israel in 1976 and from this time the house had gone into decline. Joash was a reclusive individual who did not take kindly to any offers of help, which he considered to be 'interference'.

The house was in a poor condition and although Saul and Sylvia had been cleaning the walls and floors, a strong smell of smoke hung in the air. I was told that the blackened walls and blistering paintwork of the doors and windows had been the result of a serious fire in 1999, probably caused by Joash falling asleep and dropping his tobacco pipe onto the floor. Joash had managed to escape but had insisted he should return to the smouldering house immediately afterwards. During the years leading up to the fire, both Saul and Sylvia had made regular trips from Manchester to visit Joash, in an increasingly difficult attempt to allow him to retain his personal independence. With his health declining the inevitable

Figs. 1 and 2 Drawings from the *Magazine of Art*, 1896

happened and, with the family constantly worried about his well being, he was admitted to hospital suffering from a serious infection. After extensive treatment and a lengthy recovery period he was released from hospital and moved into sheltered accommodation.

When I first cast eyes on Joash's paintings I was astonished at the quantity of work. What I could see looked fascinating but uncared for. Unknown to all at this time the collection comprised of nearly all Joash's work from his early days at Leeds Art College through to his last drawings and paintings from the mid 1990s. Paintings were piled to the ceiling and stacked tightly against the walls, making it virtually impossible to see anything of the work. Many of the oil paintings had become stuck together due to the thickness of paint and the weight of the paintings stacked on top of one another. A two foot high pile of drawings in the kitchen included at least 1,000 works, their edges scarred by the heat and dirt of the fire. Sketch books were stacked on the window sill. A few pieces of sculpture were dotted around the house; the remnants of a collection destroyed by fire. Every room was filled with work. The bare brick attic contained a mural of a figure, painted by candlelight. The garden, completely overgrown and neglected until recently, displayed shards of painted roof-tiles and slate painted by Joash. A chair, small table and stove in the front room were evidence of the few home comforts he allowed himself.

Having managed to sell Joash's collection of books, the Woodrow family were in a dilemma as to the future of Joash's work. In all the time that Joash had lived on his own at the house he had shown no interest in allowing anyone to view or discuss his paintings. For Saul and Sylvia the paintings were now proving to be a serious problem.

During the past four years Saul and Sylvia had spent most weekends travelling from Manchester to the family home in Leeds and I sensed clearly their deep concerns about Joash's welfare, his work and the dilemma it posed. How should they deal with such a vast, damaged assortment of works by a previously unknown artist? Could the paintings be sold

Figs. 3 and 4 The interior of 25 Allerton Grange Gardens, Leeds, 2000.

or should they be destroyed? As far as anyone knew Joash had never attempted to sell his paintings and few if any had been exhibited.

Saul kindly allowed me to purchase a small group of paintings to consider back at home with Gillian, my wife and business partner. Although excited by the discovery, the thought of tackling such a large and hugely speculative collection was daunting. I was as ever cautious and careful before passing judgement on what was, with hindsight, obvious – an artist of new vision in its truest, purest sense. Saul had already contacted the local art gallery to seek independent advice; little interest was shown in the work, no doubt due to the fact that the paintings were virtually impossible to view in such crowded, small spaces. Eventually a solution was agreed and it was decided to remove all of the paintings and artist's materials to a small store, where 50 works would be chosen for photography and conservation. Although cramped, the new store would provide a secure, dry home for the pictures.

Now, having an opportunity to view some individual works it became clear that the paintings spanned at least a period of 30–40 years and were obviously very personal, honest, and powerful pieces of art. With such a diversity of pictures I increasingly felt that it would be important to meet with Joash, hopefully to catch a glimpse, an insight into the maker of these works. Perhaps Joash had not discussed his art with anyone because he felt isolated from those who might understand or appreciate his talent? Had he maintained his silence so as to avoid criticism which might have damaged him as an artist?

Saul and Sylvia arranged for me to visit Joash at his new home in Manchester. Having been led into his room Saul introduced me to Joash who was sitting quietly, slightly agitated I felt, by the intrusion. During our 15 minutes or so spent together I expressed my enthusiasm for his work and asked Joash questions about his influences and his time at the Royal College. Joash was hesitant to respond and wary, avoiding eye contact, answering in concise, short sentences. At the end of our time together I asked whether he might be

Fig. 5 Saul Woodrow examining paintings in the attic at 25 Allerton Grange Gardens, 2000.
Image courtesy of the Yorkshire Post

Fig. 6 Reverse of **Self-Portrait with Pipe and Hat** (see fig. 33). Paint on darned sackcloth

Fig. 7 Cataloguing and conservation of the Woodrow books.

interested in a small exhibition of his work being held in Harrogate. At this point he stopped suddenly as though the idea had proved too much to consider. A few silent minutes passed. I thanked Joash and we left.

Returning to the conservation studio I was increasingly excited by what I was finding and keen to seek criticism from others. A selection of photographs was sent to the art critic and writer Nicholas Usherwood. His first call to me was full of enthusiasm for the works, and within a few days he had travelled to Harrogate to see the original pictures. It was one of those special moments, when his sense of genuine excitement and warmth confirmed my own beliefs that whatever happened in the future, these paintings were extraordinary and beautiful.

During the next year the conservation studio was particularly busy with the cleaning and repair of Joash's paintings; removing the thick layers of dirt to reveal the fresh colours beneath, very different to my memories of the veiled, monochrome pictures seen at the house. With time, a chronology of his technique and style slowly became apparent. His earliest oil paintings from the late 1940s until circa 1953 were usually painted on hardboard using traditional oil paints. From this time, until the death of his mother in 1961, it seems that Joash painted few paintings, although he continued to draw. He then began to paint on remnants of coarse potato and coal hessian sacking which he simply darned with wool and wire, pulling the tears together before stretching over crudely prepared strainers, made from discarded pieces of rough timber, picture frames, and even bits of tree branches. Nails used to tack the material to the strainers were left protruding, as though the urgency to complete the next canvas for his painting was all consuming. Works from the early 1970s onwards were usually executed on sheets of hardboard, allowing him access to paint on surfaces up to 8 × 5 feet. To paint on such a large scale in such cramped conditions must have proved difficult and we know that having painted on one of these boards he would leave the painting face up in the garden to dry for a while before returning it to the house for finishing. Over a period of months the thick impasto paint would often form deep wrinkles which he would sometimes re-work, emphasising the effect of the wrinkling by scraping fresh, lighter coloured paint over the tops of the ridges. From around 1970 Joash also started to add linseed stand oil to his paint, creating a beautiful rich glaze when required. Joash increasingly used commercial household paints mixed with oil paint, frequently combined with grit or sand to add body. From the ealy 1970s he began to use dry 'Rowney School Art' powder pigments, either mixed in with the paint, or on occasions sprinkled dry on to the canvas, before pouring and mixing paint on top. Many of the paintings have white chalk lines drawn on top of the paint, which he seems to have used at all stages during the development of a painting to correct or alter his composition. Although hardboard or sackcloth were by far the most frequently used supports for his paintings, Joash often used pieces of printed advertising board to paint on, sometimes allowing the printed image to shine through his painting, becoming part of the finished picture.

Once in the studio the ethical problems of conservation versus restoration posed several major questions. All of the paintings required treatment, having been affected by the years of air borne nicotine smoke and latterly the gritty soot deposits caused by the house fire. The other major problem was that posed by the 'stretchers' which Joash had used to support his paintings. Bits of crude timber and rusty nails provided poor supports for the paintings, however, having worked closely with the collection over a period of months it was considered that they formed an integral part of the paintings and that any structural restoration should be kept to a minimum.

Fig. 8 **Still Life with Jugs** Oil on metal

Fig. 9 Reverse of **Still Life with Jugs** – metal advertising board

Various methods of removing the surface dirt from the paintings were tested and eventually it was decided to remove as much dirt as possible from the paintings by vacuum suction, employing a bristle brush to agitate any stubborn ingrained areas. The remaining dirt was removed using small cotton wool swabs and a weak aqueous cleaning solution. The coarse fabric and heavy impasto made this a difficult and lengthy process, with particularly close attention paid to the areas where Joash's use of dry pigment dusted the surface of the pictures. Once remedial cleaning had been completed, most of the paintings were found to be in exceptionally good condition with few structural problems. Numerous other problems arose including how to deal with the paintings on laminated paper advertising boards and the flaking rust from the metal 'Esso Lubrication' advertising panel (fig. 9). The 2,000 works on paper also required a further conservation specialism, and it is likely that an ongoing programme of conservation will take at least a further three years to complete.

With the conservation of the paintings underway Saul agreed that we should hold a small exhibition of Joash's work in Harrogate in May 2002. As we began to hang the paintings I was charged with a great sense of excitement. Cleaned, framed and finally displayed on the walls, the paintings had taken on a life of their own with a quality to match any of his contemporaries.

As with all new artists there is usually a considerable wariness from collectors and I anticipated reservations. However on the opening night people arrived in droves with an incredible sense of urgency and excitement in the air. One collector who couldn't decide which picture to buy hid a painting behind a curtain to avoid it selling before he could make up his mind. Two others fought over yet another painting. Saul and Sylvia were encouraged with the positive response to Joash's work and it was an overwhelming success by any measure. During the following days I was delighted to meet with Joash's other brothers Paul and Joseph. Both were moved by the exhibition, having previously been unaware of the wide range of work produced by Joash. I feel that it must have been difficult for them to have absorbed the transformation. During Joash's last years in Leeds they were rarely, if ever invited to see Joash's new work. Their visit to Harrogate to view so many of these unfamiliar images, cleaned, framed and exhibited in new surroundings, being looked at and talked about by strangers, must have had a deep emotional impact. Joash remained unaware of the exhibition and the public response.

Following the success of the first Joash exhibition we continued with a programme of cataloguing, photographing and conserving the paintings and drawings. A further 50 paintings were prepared and shown the following year. This event was to prove a turning point. A prominent article in *The Times* attracted a flood of enquiries and during the following week the gallery (our home) struggled to cope with the vast number of visitors, many travelling from all parts of the UK and abroad. The phones rang constantly with calls received both night and day from collectors around the globe. During the following weeks journalists from Scandinavia, Canada, and Australia covered the story, with the gallery receiving interest from various film and programme makers. Local galleries and shops were inundated with people calling to ask where the exhibition was being held. As the week progressed it became clear that we could not deal with the volume of people coming to the

Fig. 10 View of the Joash Woodrow exhibition, Harrogate, 2002.

gallery and a security firm was employed to help control the hundreds of visitors arriving each day. This in itself proved controversial as we were told that several visitors had complained to other galleries in town that they had 'been frisked' by the security door man. Untrue; but a novel thought.

One of the greatest delights of being involved with the Joash Woodrow story has been in listening to those who have been moved by his work. The paintings have affected so many; passions have been aroused. An artist friend who has visited each of the exhibitions told me the day after the first exhibition preview that as she slept she re-visited the exhibition in her dreams, moving from room to room remembering each and every picture. Many others have experienced a similar response, retaining clear images of the paintings in their minds long after the exhibition. Experienced collectors too have frequently been surprised by the emotional impact of Joash's vision, touched by the depth of soul in the paintings.

An artist of our own time Joash spent his entire working life devoted to producing a pure and undeniably honest depiction of his thoughts and the physical world around him. Although he remains unaware of the growing interest in his work I feel that he must have believed in the incredible power of his work and of what it might eventually mean to so many others.

We did not have the luxury of watching the artist as he matured and developed. It is unlikely that Joash will ever discuss his work. There is little anecdotal reference to his personal life, his likes, dislikes, passions, artistic influences. Perhaps the best we can hope for is that his paintings will now be considered fully and that with time his contribution to art will be acknowledged.

Coming in from afar
The life and work of Joash Woodrow

Nicholas Usherwood and Christopher P. Wood

> I was filled with feelings and sensations.
> Now all that's like
> a line of dots in parenthesis
>
> Where was I hiding out
> where did I bury myself?
> Not a bad trick
> to vanish before my own eyes.
>
> Wisława Symborska from 'May 16,1973'

Writing about any artist's life and work can never be more than an approximation to the interior truths, beliefs and myths that they may choose to reveal about themselves, those elements of their life that might seem to have some relevance to their achievement and, of course, what may be inferred from the work itself. In the case of Joash Woodrow, however, we have a biography that consists essentially of no more than two or three paragraphs, the testimony of no more than four or five people who can ever remember him as an artist at any stage in his life and only one recorded personal statement about what it was that impelled him to make the 750 paintings and sculptures and several thousand drawings that lay awaiting discovery when he finally stopped working a decade or so ago. The word 'impelled' is used advisedly for, as all those who have looked carefully at the archive of his work that has been set up since 2001 will testify, there is no question of the astonishingly expressive emotional force and drive that lies behind virtually every work within it, whether an 8′ × 5′ canvas or the smallest of working sketchbooks.

And these are effectively, all we have – the inferences that can be drawn between the sparse, if intensely dramatic 'facts' of his life and the rich but often tantalisingly obscure poetry of the work itself. One fundamental point needs to be made before the process of unravelling can begin however, and how we should regard what happened at that moment in 1955 when his mother came down to London and 'recovered' her son at the onset of the mental illness that was to trouble him for the rest of his life – a moment which we can now, paradoxically, regard as marking the true beginning of his mature artistic achievement. For, however we approach his work, we cannot assess it as anything less than the deliberate manifestation of an eccentric but visually sophisticated and professionally trained artistic intelligence. The seemingly deliberate retreat into a self-imposed and intensely painful interior exile was in order to explore, without disturbance, a world complete and of itself –

Coming in from afar

an insider 'Outsider' artist almost from the very start. The extraordinary circumstances of his life and also his subsequent discovery, dramatic and often melancholy as they are, have to be seen as separate from the processes by which we can start to give Joash Woodrow his proper place within the art-history of the time.

It is only at this point, in the late 1950s, settled in the small family home in Chapel Allerton, North Leeds, with his mother and three brothers, his illness apparently under some degree of control, that Joash would appear to have begun to understand the real nature of his artistic gift, his 'voice' if you like, and how best it could be realised. His expressive roots clearly relate back to a tradition of Jewish/East European exile art that has proved an enormously powerful force in Modern British Art. Gertler, Bomberg, Kossoff, Auerbach and Freud are perhaps the best known names in this tradition but others less familiar, such as Jacob Kramer, who had come to Leeds from the Ukraine in 1900 are perhaps no less influential artistically. Kramer, for example, was a key influence on the intellectual development of the Modernist writer and critic Herbert Read (as well as being the first significant artist he had then met) dating back to the time when he was a student at the university there and had attended meetings of the Leeds Art Club. Read had remained a frequent visitor to the city in the intervening years, particularly in the post-war period while Jacob ('Jack' as he was known to artists there) Kramer was a force to be reckoned with in Leeds artistic life right up to his death in 1962.

Fig. 11 Joash's father, Harry Woodrow

Leeds, as a major centre of the tailoring industry, had drawn many East European families such as the Woodrow's (originally Wardrovsky and from Bialystok in Eastern Poland close to the Russian border) to work in its factories. Joash Woodrow's family background, however, was perhaps different from the majority of them in the depth and passion of its intellectual, political and literary culture. His father, Harry (Herzl), by training a Hebrew scholar, had come to Leeds as a teenager around 1903/4 before briefly running a Jewish bookshop in Boston (USA) for a period with his with his new wife, Rebecca (Rifka), in 1911. Returning to Leeds in 1912, they again had a bookshop, in the Chapeltown district – some of Joash's earliest surviving studies while at Leeds Art School in the late 1940s depict the building in which it was situated. When book sales failed to provide for a rapidly growing family he had finally gone to work in the tailoring industry, on the shop-floor of Sir Montague Burton's clothing factory. The profound love of books never left him despite the physical hardships of such a life, family memories are of him always quietly reading in a corner of the room, while Joash's small studies of his father also show him absorbed in a book. It seems to have been the central and significant consolation of his life; a family story records how Sir Montague Burton would come down onto the shop-floor to find him and take him back to his office to discuss what they were reading at the Leeds' book club where they were both members at the time. Interestingly, too, Sir Montague's enquiries as to why a man of such obvious gifts as Harry's would want to remain on the shop-floor rather than in management were always met with a steady rebuttal, based on the grounds that it would undermine his firmly held socialist/Trades Unionist views.

Fig. 12 Portrait of Joash's father reading

COMING IN FROM AFAR

Fig. 13 Joash's mother, Rebecca Woodrow

Fig. 14 **Portrait of the Artist's Mother**
Pencil drawing
Private collection

In these he must have shared a great deal in common with his wife Rebecca who he had first met in Leeds where she had returned to be with her family after spending some time in Palestine during the years 1906/7. By contrast Rebecca was, despite having nine children, an altogether more dynamic personality, politically very active and yet still very much the focus of family life right up to her death in 1961, ten years or so after Harry. In all of this, one senses a huge underlying pride and acknowledgement of their European/Jewish origins and the strength of their Internationalist views (two of Joash's sisters went to live and work in Palestine and, after the war, the new state of Israel). This may begin to account for the strong presence in Joash's work of a more European, at times more specifically Eastern European symbolist/modernist expression, different perhaps to the more formalist variations of the tradition adopted by Bomberg, Auerbach and other artists of the School of London.

Born in 1926, Joash was the third youngest of nine children and it is a considerable testimony to the cultural and intellectual ambition of his parents that he was one of six that went on to higher education – mathematics, economics, medicine (a professor), a production engineer and two, Joash and Paul, into art. In Joash's case a youthful enthusiasm had translated initially into studies at the art-school in Leeds in 1942, studies which were then interrupted by National Service, spent working as a cartographer with the Royal Engineers in Egypt from 1945–48. He then returned to complete his studies in Leeds where, over the next two years, he gained his School Certificate and, much more significantly, a Scholarship to the Royal College of Art which he took up in 1950. From the few surviving photographs of this period, notably those taken while he was in Egypt, the open, smiling face confirms the memories of both family and art-school friends: that there were no obvious signs of the nervous breakdown that was to overtake him during his time in London.

The artist Cyril Satorsky (now living in the USA), who studied with him in Leeds and then at the RCA, where they shared digs for a period, has recently provided a revealing picture of him from this time. He remembers how 'I enjoyed his friendship greatly in those very distant Leeds years when he still lived at home and he could be a fun person then. I exchanged many letters with him during his time in Egypt; those remote teen years were golden years.' The small group of his paintings which survive from this time are, for the most part, small-scale urban street and figure studies, painted in gouache, identifiably of the Chapeltown area of North Leeds where the family was then living and including, in at least one case, the building that had formerly housed his father's bookshop. Painted in sombre, dark-toned greys, browns and blacks, these obviously deeply felt works show Joash painting in a broadly Realist/Expressionist manner very much of its time with influences from Josef Herman through to the Euston Road School, a kind of precursor of the early Kitchen Sink realism he was soon to encounter with Bratby and others at the Royal College.

There are, at the same time, in Satorsky's account of his friendship with Woodrow, hints of a personality which may well have contributed to the nervous breakdown he suffered soon after leaving the RCA in 1953. 'He was always of a shy nature and never outgoing as a person. As a friend he was always sweet and sensitive but there was an intensity about him that closed him off from freely moving among other students and participating with any ease in social events, even of a light or casual kind. It's my impression (hindsight obviously) that he must have suffered from depression from his teen years on. I think he was lonely at the RCA and in London generally.... I believe these days he would be described as a "loner". ... it was something of a mystery what he did with his time.' There is a hint, too, according to Satorsky's an account of his being 'sweet on a girl (not Jewish) but doubt if he ever approached her' and sufficient expression of annoyance and anger when Satorsky had raised the subject for him not to pursue it again.

Given the difficulties already alluded to, as well as the fact that he only very rarely ever signed or dated his work, and exhibition labels are few and far between, establishing any kind of precise chronology of his work is difficult. What kind of work Joash was doing while he was actually at the RCA other than life drawing is almost impossible to surmise. The chances are that very little survived that moment *ca.*1955 when his mother took Joash and his few possessions back home to Leeds. Perhaps something can be inferred from those works that appear to have been started in the years immediately after his return, works which can be linked with a landscape study inscribed 'S. Kensington' on the reverse and the only painting which can be certainly dated to his Royal College years. For the most part landscape studies, *Boat on a Shore* (fig. 18), *Twilight Street* (fig. 19) and *Rural Landscape with Buildings* (fig. 20) are all brooding, dark-toned oils, all painted directly onto masonite. In each of them the subject of the painting – a building, a boat or a chimney take on a ghostly and intangible quality, fusing organically into the landscape like something that has grown rather than been built. In *Rural Landscape with Buildings*, for example, a darkly outlined building is flanked by the flaying branches of the trees, giving the impression that it is about to explode. And, though the colour in these works has grown stronger and more chromatic compared to the Leeds cityscapes of the late 1940s, these new intense blues, turquoise greens, yellow ochres and flashes of red-gold and carmine pinks, nonetheless reflect a sombre and distant soul.

In the surviving portraits that can be linked stylistically with these landscapes, the same weighty, impenetrable vision is pursued, with the figures and faces emerging from darkness rather than from light, the colours again rich and brooding. In one of the finest of these

Fig. 15 Joash in Egypt, 1948

Fig. 16 **Dark Landscape**
Oil on board   *circa* 1950–1955

Fig. 17 **Tree, with Buildings Beyond**
Oil on board   *circa* 1955–1960

Fig. 18 **Boat on a Shore**
Oil on board, *circa* 1955–1960
Private collection

Fig. 19 **Twilight Street**
Oil on board, *circa* 1955
Private collection

heads, *Portrait of a Young Man* (fig. 21), the structure of the bold, dark forms is illuminated by gleams of petrol blue, carmine pink, turquoise and even gold, the almost iconic, religious solemnity of the feeling it conveys, not unlike the work of the French Fauvist painter Georges Rouault in both its subject and effect.

In all these works it is worth commenting finally on their comparatively small scale. Following his return home, these works would have been painted in the very cramped spaces of the house in Allerton Grange Gardens, but this may even have been the way he tended to work while at the RCA, preferring to paint at home in his digs rather than in the huge, almost intimidating spacious Victorian studios of the Henry Cole building in South Kensington that then housed the Painting Schools.

Commenting on his painting style while at the College, Satorsky observed that 'his colour and compositional sense I always thought had a very dramatic and taut quality. I particularly liked his landscapes – there was something Fauv-ish about his manipulation of paint that gave it a rich, fat quality.' Satorsky adds, almost as a footnote, how he thought 'the professors at the RCA found him remote and distant and not very responsive'. This last opinion is a harder one to assess half a century on. Tutors, Carel Weight, Ruskin Spear, and Robert Buhler, who all gave him such glowing testimonials are long since dead while Colin Hayes (who died in 2003), when asked, had no memory of him of any kind. There was a similar response from many of the artists who had been fellow students, not one of whom, when asked, had any recollection of his name. All of this tends to confirm the feeling that he did not make any particular impact on anyone while he was there, though given the intensely social and competitive nature of the College at the time, and Joash's shy and retiring nature, not too much should be read into any of this. However, Joash recently remarked to Andrew Stewart, that Robert Buhler had visited Woodrow's RCA studio on a few occasions

Fig. 20 **Rural Landscape with Buildings**
Oil on board, *circa* 1955–1960

and had observed that he painted more like a European than an English artist – a remark of some insight and significance in the light of the way his work was to develop over the next two decades or so. To summarise, none of this makes for an exceptional story; the College in those days saw plenty of gifted, working class provincial students come through its doors – a few succeeded but many more were never heard of again as artists. While Joash may not have been well remembered, the fact that he did not finally become one of that latter group is, in the end, down to the unquestionable intellectual gifts, artistic drive and instinct

Fig. 21 **Portrait of a Young Man**
Oil on board, *circa* 1955–1960
Private collection

Fig. 22 **Portrait of a Man Wearing a Hat**
Oil on sackcloth, *circa* 1955–1960

Fig. 23 **Portrait of Satorsky**
Oil on sackcloth, *circa* 1960
Private collection

Fig. 24 **The Yellow House**
Oil on board, *circa* 1955–1960.

Fig. 25 **The White Gate**
Oil on board, *circa* 1955–1960
Private collection

for survival which compelled him to seize on the lifeline thrown to him by his family in 1955.

His situation at that point, a year or so out of college and working apparently as an accountant and quite possibly not painting very much as a consequence, must, for someone of Joash's patently explosive but fragile and introverted artistic temperament, have seemed intolerably frustrating. The return to Leeds on the other hand, to a safe, familiar environment with everyday anxieties offset by the lifelong financial support his family was able to provide, gave him the kind of emotional stability and independence that enabled him to return to painting and start on that process of developing at his own pace largely free from the outside pressures that might normally hinder artistic development.

His immediate environment may not have been so easy in the first few years back in Leeds. The house at 25 Allerton Grange Gardens was a relativly small post-war semi-detached house with a small living room dining room and kitchen on the ground floor and three small bedrooms upstairs, shared between Joash, his mother and two brothers. It is this space, or rather the lack of it, that accounts for the generally small scale of the works from this first period back in the family home, the large 4′ × 3′ canvas that he painted of his mother resting being the rare exception, a precursor of the increasingly large-scale paintings he was to embark on after his mother's death in 1961. Then, as Paul Woodrow relates elsewhere so vividly, with just the three brothers in the house, one at work all day and the other at art-school, Joash seems to have taken over the whole of the ground floor space as his studio. The illness and depression of his London years seems to have started lifting steadily once settled back in Leeds and by the late 1950s his life seemingly revolved around painting, sketching trips to the coast and surrounding countryside with occasional visits to York and Harrogate to draw. By 1957 he was sufficiently restored to health to take the 16 year-old Paul

Fig. 26 **Crown Place, Harrogate**
Oil on board, *circa* 1980

on a trip to Paris. There they sketched the city, drew Les Deux Magots on the Boulevarde St. Germaine, looking for Sartre. Certainly, judging by the extremely wide range of references to European contemporary art movements to be found in his dissertation at the RCA and from the range of reading, theatre-going and preferred listening that Paul Woodrow's account conveys, Joash comes across as enlightened and familiar with contemporary developments in European artistic and philosophical thought, as well as leading a rich and varied cultural life.

For all this activity it seems that he never developed any close friendships outside his family, his relationship with Paul, always close, becoming even more so in the years immediately after his mother's death. Indeed, it was Paul's friends, Peter Doefler, the writer Danny Padmore and Paul's wife to be, Judith Allin who, for the most part, provided the principal models for Joash's growing interest in portraits. Some of his earliest surviving drawings are portraits made of his father and mother, done when he was 14 or 15 years old, while the *Portrait of a Young Man in a White Striped Top* (fig. 27) from the mid-1950s, shows him working in a powerful late Cezanne-esque manner, still essentially concerned with capturing a likeness. Well executed but still comparatively conventional in character there is no advance warning in these works of the remarkable way they were to develop between now and the late 1970s. Exploding with energy and rich in experimentation, they show him embarking on

COMING IN FROM AFAR

Fig. 27 **Portrait of a Young Man in a White Striped Top**
Oil on board, *circa* 1955–1960
Private collection

perhaps one of the most powerfully individualistic and original series of portraits in post-war British art.

The catalyst for this expressive outpouring was undoubtedly 'Fifty Years of Picasso' an exhibition held at the Tate Gallery in 1960, which Joash visited several times with his brother Paul. The impact this show had on him seemed to coincide with an abrupt change in his artistic language and a new understanding of materials and how he wanted to use them. Up to this point the surface quality of the paintings had only been a by-product of his struggle to release his images and not part of his central concern. Now everything seemed different, as if his Jewish heritage had suddenly begun to take on a new significance for him, his Eastern European culture energised by the realisation that his expressive roots lay outside the British Isles. It was as if he had just rediscovered the source of those creative energies that were to carry him through the next 35 years of artistic activity. And it was not only Picasso but a whole range of contemporary European movements that now seemed to become relevant to his needs. Dubuffet and Art Brut, with its blistering, raw paint surfaces, Appel, Jorn, Constant and the COBRA group with a radically Expressionist style of painting, quite unlike anything seen in this country, De Staël, Soulages and the Tachistes with their insistence on the quality of the mark-making and the Indian painter F. N. Souza whose 1960 exhibition at Cartwright Hall, Bradford, he would have probably visited. All have their bearing on this dawning realisation of the real character of his artistic direction. It is very much the same for his drawing, where, the graphic 'bite' of the pencil lends such a force, a quality that was to distinguish almost every one of the drawings he made over the next 40 years or more.

These radically changed attitudes can be seen in the kinds of materials he now selected for painting – the roughest sackcloth, hessian and canvas; discarded bits of wood and old picture frames crudely and impatiently nailed together to make the stretchers, using house paints, ripolin enamel, varnish, raw pigments and sawdust as the preferred media. It is a whole world away from his previous techniques as gesture and surface texture rapidly become as important to his expressive means as image and likeness. The portrait too now takes on an entirely different quality, as can be seen in the two portraits of Gilbert (see pages 48, 49), where he succeeds in achieving an exquisite balance between the raw crudity of the sackcloth surface and the tentative, delicately brushed black outline describing the downcast face of the sitter. Elsewhere the paint-dripped features of a man in tears, delicate, poetic and full of pain, give this work a claim to be one of his most memorable portraits. In each of these works the accuracy with which he renders detail, such as the young man's stubbly beard for example, with such apparently crude materials is, quite simply, astonishing.

Two other strands of exploration also start to emerge in the early to mid 1960s, notably the continuing development of the landscape themes, together with an exploration of all his subjects through a Picasso-inspired Modernism. The landscapes start to reflect the massive amount of drawing that Joash was now making as part of his daily activity. This first becomes apparent as, slowly and deliberately, he begins to break down the landscape into more distinct graphic, linear forms. *White House in a Landscape* (fig. 28) is a pivotal piece in this respect, in which the dark forms of the tree and branches are broken down and painted with short, angular brushstrokes that flatten out the top part of the painting. This process continues in paintings like *Monochrome Landscape* (fig. 29) in which the picture becomes a flattened sequence of lines that threaten to bury the house and the whole subject of the painting beneath them! Gradually, however, in a series of quite brilliantly inventive paintings, Joash succeeds in simplifying the picture plane into a progression of broad, regular brushstrokes which step, glide and dance across the picture plane, overlaying and framing flat areas of colour which suggest the subject of the painting. *Landscape with Black Tree* and *Abstract Landscape* (fig. 30), both dating from around 1966–69 (as far as can be deduced from the few signed and dated pieces we have of this period), show this new vision of the landscape in its most fully realised form.

This period seems generally to have been a happy and productive time for Joash. A number of recorded paintings were sent to open submission exhibitions – the enigmatically entitled *He also Fights for a Free World* to the Cartwright Hall Open show in Bradford in 1965, and others to the John Moores in Liverpool in 1967 (also in 1972) and the Edinburgh Open in 1969 but none, as far as we can tell, were accepted. Joash's work, with its values

Fig. 28 **White House in a Landscape**
Oil on board, *circa* 1960–1965

Fig. 29 **Monochrome Landscape**
Oil on board, *circa* 1960–1965

Fig. 30 **Abstract Landscape**
Oil on board, *circa* 1966–1969

deeply rooted in European Art of the 1930s and 1940s, would have been unlikely to have found much favour in the face of the massive upheavals in artistic taste and fashion engendered first by Pop Art and American post-painterly abstraction in the early 1960s and then by the burgeoning Conceptual Movement, that was to develop with great energy and force in the late part of the decade. It marks the moment at which he starts slowly to withdraw from the art-world, his John Moores submission in 1972 almost certainly his last. Why we can only guess: an acute dislike and fear of rejection, common to most artists; an impatience with the expense and palaver of packing and transporting work, or simply a wish just to get on with the work free of distraction. Or, perhaps, elements of all these things combined with the increasing isolation of his life after Paul married in 1967 and emigrated soon after to Canada. It marks the first stage in the story of his long retreat in to the enclosed, painting-obsessed world that defines his life from the mid 1970s onwards, a retreat that, paradoxically, was to result in the most exuberant, extrovert and original work of his career.

Somewhere towards the end of this period Joash, still using the same broad brushstrokes and flattened pictorial space used in the landscapes, also seems to have started a series of luminous, semi-abstract still lives. In these works he seems more concerned with the actual surface quality of the paintings and, while still using the same kind of sackcloth sewn together as a support, he starts exploring, in an almost playful manner, the dynamics of composition and materials to produce some startlingly original works. *Still Life with White Bowl and Cake* (fig. 31) for example, is extraordinary for the sheer range of devices Joash employed to apply paint; as well as a wide number of specialist and commercially available brushes, he improvises with scrapers, squeegees and uses the handles of his brushes to scrape through the congealing paint. In this picture too, he drops raw, dry pigment into the still wet surface, mimicking the icing sugar dusted on the cake in the centre right of the painting before scratching through the paint to give an indication of how it was decorated. What makes this painting so particularly interesting is the dynamic balance he achieves between the naturalistic linear perspective of the table, the blue knives, the plate on which the cake sits and even the jug at the back of the table, which all follow the normal rules of perspective, while the left-hand side of the composition and the bowl of fruit at the back are completely flattened, their shapes abstracted for the purpose of its overall design. The juxtaposition of different spaces within one painting is not, of course, unique in modern art but it is, nevertheless, used with a very considerable power of expression and visual sophistication of a kind that is not that common in British art of the post-war period.

It is, in short, a complex artistic personality that is beginning to develop by the end of the 1960s; from what we know of him from family and friends and from his writings as revealed in his RCA thesis entitled 'Art and Epigonism,' he had a highly intelligent, well-informed mind. At the same time it is an artistic intelligence, expressed in often urgent, compulsive, sometimes distinctly forceful terms. Outwardly he would seem to have been a shy, sensitive and somewhat withdrawn figure and yet also quick to anger. It conjures up an

Fig. 31 **Still Life with White Bowl and Cake**
Oil on hessian, *circa* 1965–1970
Private collection

Fig. 32 **Athlete**
Oil on board, *circa* 1970
Private collection

intriguing image of him at this period, painting by the fire and sucking away on his habitual pipe, one that has the sense of a smouldering volcano. It is the kind of contrast to be found in so many paintings of around this time, most particularly perhaps in the savage but tender humour of his animal paintings such as *White Goat*, *Black Bird* or *Artist and Bird*.

The more Picasso inspired themes that provide one of the main strands in his work during the 1970s already seemed to have started taking shape towards the end of the 1960s. *Knight on Horseback and Gladiator* 1969 is one of the last signed and dated works we have but it indicates that it must have been a compositional language he had been exploring alongside the landscapes and still-lives of this period. Some confirmation of this is also provided by a group of paintings based on Sidney Nolan's various 'Ned Kelly' series (often on show in London during these years), the only surviving example of which (datable from a label on the reverse) is sadly fire-damaged.

In the decade that follows Joash moves from subject to subject. Peter Doefler, a friend of Paul, whom he was using as a model at this time, gives a vivid impression of life at 25 Allerton Grange Gardens during this period, occupied as it was by the three brothers: 'I used to call round for Paul; he was a couple of years older than me but we were friends. Joash would be painting by the fire downstairs and he had the whole room, but it was already starting to fill up with paintings. The house was pretty shambolic . . . . One day Joash asked me if he could paint my picture and would I come that evening, which I did. A few days later he gave me the picture and that was that. I asked why he had chosen me, had I a particularly interesting face?' Joash's answer, one of the very few anecdotes we have, was that, if he ever 'chose to exhibit the picture he didn't want a J Brown or S Jones for a title, Doefler had a much better ring to it!' And there is an extremely revealing episode following on from this because, unknown to Doefler, Joash had produced another four substantial portraits of him, all of which remained unseen for thirty years, witness both to the extreme speed and urgency with which he worked and the intense focus of his attention in exploring every variation and nuance the subject could provide. The same concentration is apparent in the sketchbooks of these years, where he would take a subject or visit a location and make up to a dozen good size drawings in a day, as though he had to carve or etch the scene on to his visual memory.

When his brother Israel died in 1978 Joash, now living on his own, quickly seems to have filled the available space with paintings and started on a series of large-scale single and dual figure compositions which often conceptualise and reduce the human form down to flat geometric planes and shapes. *Symbolic Man* and *Two Figures* are typical examples; using the largest sheets of hardboard he could buy, he would begin by using a standard grey primer and then divide the surface up into quarters which he would then paint different shades and colours in order to give himself a solid starting point and something to work his composition against, a process often used by painters to provoke the imagination. Once this process was complete Joash would drag the large boards outside to the small rear garden to dry before dragging them back inside, usually the kitchen, to paint. Many of these large canvases have grass stuck to them or embodied on the texture of the paint, an accidental element in the work that he would certainly not have objected to. It was an indication of his determination and lack of compromise that he wanted to work on this large scale despite such physically difficult circumstances. *Artist and Bird* is part of a huge diptych showing an artist (a painter, now dead, called Peter Hibson) painting a mother and child in the garden – the weather is warm, the artist wearing his sandals, the palette on his lap. It has a distinct element of self-parody about it too, and like so many of his paintings, is full of wit and dark humour.

By the end of the decade Joash's life was becoming increasingly isolated and although Paul and his wife were still visitors (as were his two other brothers Joseph, Saul and his wife Sylvia), he was now, more and more, living in a very interior world. By the mid 1970s he was also developing his interests in collage and sculpture. The 'amended' 7 volumes of the Victorian 'Magazine of Art' (which were to become so instrumental in the story of his rediscovery) were started *ca.*1974/5 though unfortunately much of the sculpture was a victim of the fire in 2000. From the few examples that have survived they show a constructivist or,

Fig. 33 **Self-Portrait with Pipe and Hat**
Oil on sackcloth, *circa* 1970

Fig. 34 **Self-Portrait with Pipe**
Oil on board, *circa* 1965

in the case of the piano that he took apart and then re-jigged, a deconstructionist approach, that bears close comparison to his use of collage in a whole series of extraordinarily inventive and substantial works on paper from these years. Portraiture as a theme declines as his isolation (and thus lack of new sitters) grows though there are some wonderfully sharp, even savage recollections of friends and acquaintances including particularly brash pictures of his old art-school friend Satorsky.

The last figure subjects seem to have been started during the latter half of the 1970s and provide three distinctive sub-themes – a series of strange, magical or costumed groups of up to four figures, a theatrical Greco-Roman theme with athletes running, dancing and throwing javelins, while the last depicts a group of friends enjoying a day in the country with figures seated on the grass in a relaxed and informal manner. In the first a strange top-hatted figure, often only seen as a dark silhouette, haunts compositions which seem to draw their inspiration from sketches he made at the many fairs, carnivals and circuses that still regularly appear throughout the year in the suburbs of North Leeds. The top-hatted figure is often painted in a rather different manner to the rest of the group, tempting one to speculate on an autobiographical element to it. His notebooks are full of references to these events, with drawings of musicians playing concerts of classical or rock music. The second group, on the other hand, have a distinctly strange and surreal character, with echoes of De Chirico, quite unlike anything he had attempted before. The ideas may have been inspired by something seen at first hand in the theatre, or from literary sources, the radio or newspapers. In the third group, though painted with his characteristic dynamic force, the concern seems less with the overall surface quality, though the line is still invested with a remarkably wide range of expressive qualities.

By the end of the decade Joash seems to have abandoned figure painting of any description in favour of a re-investigation of his immediate surroundings, his attention focusing on the structure and light industrial and the suburban landscape of the housing and allotments he could see from the rear windows of 25 Allerton Grange Gardens. Drawings of the East Coast, signed and dated 1979, possibly of Whitby, indicate that his observation of these familiar landscapes had already begun.

By the beginning of the 1980s Joash was living alone at Allerton Grange Gardens and any documentary or anecdotal detail of his life becomes scarce as he became an increasingly isolated and solitary figure. With no one else left to sit for a portrait he began to focus his energies into literally thousands of drawings of his surroundings. The sheer number he produced at this time suggests that he must have been out and about almost every day, taking in every significant detail of the city, and more particularly the suburbs of North Leeds with which he was, by now, so familiar. He was, in effect, building up a head of steam, compiling a huge visual store of odd-shaped buildings, chimneys, picket fences, water towers, tower blocks and square modernist architectural forms, which became the elemental shapes and features that would occupy his imagination for this last creative phase of his life. Significantly they may prove to be his most original contribution to post-war British Art. Very few painters one can think of have produced such an original vision of the urban and light industrial landscape in this country in the second half of twentieth century. Joash

Fig. 35 **Cityscape with Two White Clouds**
Oil on board, *circa* 1970

sought out the square, featureless blocks of flats, offices and warehouses and used them as a backdrop against which he played the natural forms of the landscape in which they had originally been built, trees often jabbing up from the ground like naturalised telegraph poles, small white clouds bobbing along on the breeze butt up against the stark, modernist facades of the functional new architecture. *Cityscape with Two White Clouds* (fig. 35) and *Autumnal Trees in a City Landscape* are particularly fine examples of this new and powerfully original vision of our everyday landscape, making us see it as if for the first time, the mark, surely of any artist of real poetic vision. This is particularly true of the many landscapes which feature the allotments close to his home, the hotchpotch of potting-sheds and temporary structures, scrubby trees and bushes well suited to his sophisticated technique and formal inventiveness. That this is a period of artistic rejuvenation for him is apparent everywhere in the work, with blue skies abounding. *Spring Garden Landscape* is a very characteristic example, a tender and joyful work, so full of sunshine and light that you can almost hear the birds he so often liked to paint singing unseen in the trees! These works contrast so profoundly with the almost impenetrable barrier of physical and mental isolation that Joash was gradually drawing around himself in these years, the exuberant love of the everyday beauty of the world they describe can seem almost unbearably painful at times. It is as though, in these landscapes, Joash is drawing together all the experience of his previous artistic achievements, the simplifications of the mid to late 1960s, the intuitive understanding of surface and the graphic, structural power derived from many years of almost continual drawing; the final summation of his artistic vision. Among the most complex and subtly difficult of his works, they possess, paradoxically, a fundamental simplicity that marks out Joash Woodrow as an artist of extreme sophistication, proving that isolation can, and often does, strengthen an artist's conviction and sharpen his visual wits through the focus it allows on the inward eye.

For all this outpouring of new creative vision, the beginning of the 1990s also marks the moment when, though still full of great artistic energy and spirit Joash's physical and mental condition started to deteriorate with sudden and alarming consequences, to the point where one senses painting becomes something that can no longer be borne, let alone executed. The house was now so full of paintings that movement from room to room could only be negotiated through the tight corridors left between the stacks of paintings. Everything in sight was covered with the patina of nicotine from his continual pipe smoking and conditions were so cramped that that there was hardly any room left in which to paint. Joash himself had become very touchy and argumentative; one of the locals, having been invited in and giving a negative opinion, was marched out of the house and then mercilessly lampooned, as a dinosaur and other beasts, in dozens of drawings and at least one significant painting. Subsequently, if he passed the house, Joash would rush out and berate him loudly. By 1995/6 Joash's major work was completed; now 70 years old and worn out by his efforts, his mental and physical health was by now so poor it made painting and drawing an impossibility, however willing the spirit. He simply stopped, the rest of his story becoming that of sad decline and the extraordinary rediscovery documented elsewhere in this book.

The close study of this remarkable man's work over the last three years fills one with a growing admiration for the sheer personal courage, determination and force of will he needed to see his vision through to its final and intensely individual end. Continually battling with mental illness and without a network of critical or artistic support, he kept producing a steady flow of work that was distinguished, at all times, by a profound honesty and clear poetic, a committed and sensitive artist from the very start, aware from the moment he returned to Leeds that he would have to set his sights on the long haul

Fig. 36 **Edge of a Field**
Pencil on paper, signed and dated 15.5.79

Fig. 37 **Railway Embankment**
Pencil on paper, *circa* 1979

Fig. 38 **Self-Portrait**
Pencil on paper, *circa* 1975

that marks out the work of any substantial artist. Art-historians will want to assess and pigeon-hole his achievement within the framework of Modern British Art; perhaps that is the wrong approach. For the more one considers the work the more it appears as a strange and deeply intriguing outcrop of a European artistic imagination rather than a purely British sensibility.

The precise nature of his place within this more European context is hard to define at this very early stage in the process of rediscovery; the first major exhibitions, of his landscapes at Leeds City Art Gallery in 2004, and the large touring retrospective that will follow in 2005/6, will most certainly make this a great deal easier to establish. Joash was asked recently by one of his brothers what had made him paint. He paused before answering: 'it was just that it gave me great pleasure.' For the moment, it is perhaps enough for us to simply celebrate the moment of re-emergence into the world of a unique artist who had seemingly almost entirely hidden himself from view, an artist who makes us see with a fresh and tender intensity of vision.

A brother's story

Saul Woodrow

When Joash returned sometime in the mid fifties to the family home in Leeds, I was already married and living in Manchester. The consequence of this was that, until my wife Sylvia and I commenced regular visits in the early nineties to ensure Joash's well being, we had little knowledge of the style and manner of his paintings. By that time all the rooms and even the hallway had become crammed with his work to such an extent that it was impossible to view them. The opportunity was further limited by Joash's insistence that we should not move them and we found ourselves being confined to keeping the kitchen and bathroom in some state of reasonable cleanliness, disposing of the accumulated broadsheet newspapers that he so avidly read and making a visit to the local supermarket. It was during this period that Joash often spoke about an acquaintance with whom he had become angry during a discussion on Modern and Classical Art. Joash became so obsessed about it that it made those last few years in Leeds very difficult for him. Previously I had only known Joash as a quiet, gentle, calm man, and it was upsetting for the family to see this change. Today most of that rage has gone and his manner more like the brother I recall, even to occasionally displaying a touch of wry humour. There are images in his sketchbook and several of his ink drawings that show a dragon-like human, which may have been attempts to purge those negative thoughts.

Our help was only accepted with a degree of reluctance, other assistance offered by the local authority being firmly rejected. It was only when the house was being cleared after Joash entered St James's Hospital and the general consensus was that he should enter a care home on his discharge, that the full realisation of the problem became apparent. In order to calm his concerns as to the eventual fate of his lifetime's work, we promised to ensure that they would not be destroyed. That promise, which on several occasions was almost on the verge of being broken and had caused us so much worry, was, only through a series of almost unbelievable coincidences, one we were finally able to keep. The first step in that chain of events, not mentioned elsewhere, was that the seven Victorian books in which Joash had drawn over the existing plates were never intended to have been included in the consignment sent to the Harrogate bookshop. Joash had shown a specific concern that they should be retained along with his paintings but fortunately, as it transpired, they were accidentally included among the books sent to Harrogate, to be discovered by Christopher Wood.

In the early years living together in the family home, and with only eighteen months separating us in age, I must confess to feeling a degree of jealousy of the drawing skills which came so naturally to Joash. There were some advantages however in that he was expert in making very detailed model military planes and warships out of scrap materials, few commercial products being available in those austere wartime years. Dominos and Ludo

Fig. 39 **Woman with a Red Hat and Ringlets**
Oil on canvas, *circa* 1965
Private collection

Fig. 40 Joash Woodrow in Cairo, *circa* 1948.

and whilst I cannot mention them by name even several very popular copyright board games also fell to his talents.

In Joash's later dark years the feeling of jealousy changed to one of sorrow that the success his talent had promised never came. That recognition has come so late in his advancing years when he is unable or unwilling to comprehend his own achievement, may to many of us appear tragic, though Joash's own recent comment 'That he found pleasure in his painting', may be viewed as a somewhat bitter sweet consolation. Joash was not informed of the first exhibition as we had been advised that he might not be able to cope with the situation, having previously even firmly rejected the idea that his work should be cleaned and framed. He was told later that just a few carefully selected people had been allowed to view them and they were full of praise and admiration for his work. Whilst we were all a little hopeful that it might recreate some positive interest in his work it unfortunately seemed to have little effect. Since the two further highly successful exhibitions in Harrogate and the extraordinary reception given them, further hints have been made to him in the hope that he might be persuaded to visit the next one. Joash's many varied, often enigmatic images of his world displayed in this book more than compensate us for any family obligations that we may have observed and we hope that you also find the same pleasure in his work.

Growing up with Joash
Some observations about his work

Paul Woodrow

I feel truly indebted to Joash. Without him I am certain that I would not be doing what I am doing today. Teaching art and practising it. And also playing music. I feel fortunate.

Writing from memory is very much like drawing from memory in that it is a constructive act. The following account is what I choose to remember.

Hamilton Avenue

My earliest recollections of Joash are of him working in his studio at 31 Hamilton Avenue in Chapeltown. This would be in the late forties. At that time Leeds was a typical northern industrial working-class town with its factories and its dark soot stained Victorian buildings, such as the Town Hall and the Corn Exchange. A landscape often depicted in the Social Realist films of the fifties: 'Room at the Top' and 'Billy Liar' for instance; invariably shot in black and white. On the tops of trams, working men in flat caps smoked 'Woodbines', peering down through yellowing windows. In the grimy office buildings, business men wore dark suits, shiny through over wear. And in the street outside our house, there was always a smell of the carbolic soap, used to clean the front steps.

I slept in the attic next to Joash's studio – a very small room with little good light during the day. At night the street outside was still lit with gas lamps.

I have two distinct memories about the studio, both to do with smell. Firstly, the smell of turpentine and linseed oil and secondly, the rich sweet smell of Old Holborn tobacco. Though I don't now recall the kind of pictures he was painting.

When Joash returned from military service in Egypt he brought with him many exotic souvenirs, including a book of prints depicting Egyptian gods. The images were particularly beautiful, each one separated by a sheet of tissue paper, as if to denote their specialness. I also remember the cartography paper that Joash used and which he also gave me to paint on. In fact I still possess a painting that I did of the Kremlin in 1946 or 1947, executed on mapping paper.

I have a clear memory of Joash standing on the landing, humming tunes from Beethoven's symphonies. He would always test my memory. I usually did pretty well.

We would often go to hear the Yorkshire Symphony Orchestra at the Town Hall. I was quite young and I began to develop a passion for all kinds of music. We also went to the opera and the ballet. I can remember going to see Stravinsky's 'Petrouchka' around this

Fig. 41 A postcard of Joash Woodrow in Egypt, circa 1948.

time. Joash was not only struck by the music but was very impressed by the costumes. We went not only to the opera, but to a number of plays as well: 'Waiting for Godot', 'The Caretaker', and Jean Anouilh's 'The Lark'. One performance that left a deep impression on us both was that of the Indian Dancer Ram Gopal and his ensemble. Again Joash responded to the costumes and especially to the gestures of the dancers, which he found very expressive.

In the Woodrow household we were always surrounded by books, with a wide range of subject matter; from classical writers to modern novelists like James Joyce, including scientific literature, biographies, books on philosophy and many books written in Yiddish, not to mention a great variety of art books. The Woodrows, in fact, opened the first Yiddish bookstore in Leeds at the bottom of Chapeltown road close to Sheepscar.

Radio also played an important part in the household. Even as a boy I remember listening to the Third Programme of the BBC with its difficult and obscure offerings of music and plays, as well as 'The Critics', an arts review programme which came on every Sunday about noon.

I remember going with Joash on a visit to the Leeds Art Gallery, where an astounding equestrian painting by Rembrandt was on view. Leeds Art Gallery had a substantial collection of art works, from Victorian paintings to contemporary British Abstract Paintings, including the work of Terry Frost, Matthew Smith, Harold Gilman and Jack Kramer. I think that Joash quite liked the works by Kramer and Gilman. He also made me aware of Graham Sutherland's paintings too. In fact there may have been a Sutherland on display in the gallery at that time. I don't really remember having a discussion with Joash about these particular works, although I am quite certain that things were said.

We also made several trips to Temple Newsham where there were Picasso prints on display and a sculpture by Henry Moore that many people disliked intensely. Joash particularly admired the work of Jacob Epstein, the Jewish sculptor from Leeds and I remember him taking me to a building in London to show me one of Epstein's works. I think it was near to Victoria station.

Fig. 42 **Mr Woodrow's Bookshop, Chapeltown Road, Leeds.**
Gouache on paper, circa 1945
Private collection

Paris

In the mid fifties we went to Paris by train. When we arrived we tried to find a hotel near the Rue Pigalle. And I remember Joash knocking on the door of what I presumed was a hotel and a young woman answered the door, took one look at me and said something in French like…

'He is underage. We cannot let him enter'.

At the time of course, I wasn't exactly sure what the problem was.

On another occasion we bought some cheese and a baguette from the local 'alimentation' and when we got back to the hotel and opened the cheese, we thought it was mouldy and threw it away. It was of course 'Camembert'. Though both knowledgable and sophisticated in our understanding of art, we were clearly more typically 'Northern' when it came to food.

In Paris we acted like artists, strolling around La Place du Tetre in Montmartre, sketching and painting, drinking coffee at the Cafe de Flore and Les Deux Magots on the left Bank, whilst looking for Jean-Paul Sartre and other famous literary figures, who I'm sure we would not have been able to recognise even if we'd seen them. We visited the Louvre, the Jeu de Paume, the Orangerie. We drank wine from the bottle, ate baguettes and cheese, sitting by the Seine.

I remember how great it felt. Paris always smelt different; a combination of Gaullois cigarettes, perfume and urine smells, that were definitely not commonplace in Leeds of the nineteen fifties.

Fig. 43 **Le Bistro**
Oil on sackcloth, *circa* 1960–1965
Private collection

London

In 1960 we visited the Picasso exhibition at the Tate a number of times and we were very impressed by the diversity of his work, which included paintings, collages and sculptures. And in a small gallery, at Zwemmer's Art Book Shop, we saw an exhibition of Picasso's ceramic work. It was all overwhelming.

That evening we went to a Promenade concert at the Royal Albert Hall. One of the 'Beethoven nights', enjoying both the music of Sixth Symphony, and the experience of being part of the 'Promenade'.

We also visited the National Gallery and the British Museum, but it was a painting by Sidney Nolan, the Australian painter, that Joash seemed most taken with. It was one of the 'Ned Kelly' series. And he was very struck by the contrast between the metal mask (which to him was almost cubistic) and the naturalistic treatment of the figure. Joash used a similar approach in later paintings based on Nolan's 'Ned Kelly'.

Fig. 44 Cover of the Picasso exhibition catalogue. Tate Gallery, 1960

Allerton Grange Gardens

In the early sixties Joash returned to Leeds to live in a small semi-detached house in Allerton Grange Gardens. At that time there were four of us living there; myself, Izzy, Joash and mother.

With the exception of two very small bedrooms, Joash's work began to occupy the whole house. Gradually every room – the dining room, the front room – began to fill up with assortments of drawings, paintings and sculptures. Joash even used the loft as a storage place.

In the front room there was an old piano, the one on which I taught myself to play jazz – encouraged by my brother Saul – and which Joash also occasionally played. This piano was eventually taken apart by Joash and reassembled as a series of sculptures. I am not sure what happened to the iron frame. Maybe this is just my imagination, as we had a number of pianos over the years.

Whilst living at 25 Allerton Grange Gardens I was able to witness Joash at work, although this was only for a short period of time. It occurs to me now that he preferred to work in solitude and usually at night.

It seems that he was very much under the influence of Picasso at this time. Particularly in the representation of figures and his use of a blue/grey palette. One favourite painting, he told me, was 'The Three Musicians'. What I have always admired about Joash's work are the surfaces he creates, the materials he employs. Again, it is the smells that are particularly evocative for me: the under-painting, sizing the canvas, rabbit glue spread over masonite, the oils and the turpentine.

At that time Joash used a variety of paints to make his work, which included traditional mediums and oils; but he also used house paints and enamels. He particularly liked to use enamel paint for the colour – he would often use additional materials; grit, sawdust and possibly sand, to give his painting a much more physical presence, rather than the look of a thinly veiled image. The painting always felt quite heavy and dense as well as being *literally*

Fig. 45 **Moon Dancers**
Collage, *circa* 1968
Private collection

heavy, especially when they had to be moved from the dining room to the front room. He also worked with a variety of implements, not always brushes bought at the art supply store, but sticks, mops, trowels and scrapers. He'd often use bits of sacking that he had found, goodness knows where, or he would come home carrying pieces of a poster, rolls of wallpaper, or some coloured scraps of cardboard that he had picked up somewhere. Even part of a chair leg.

He also liked to paint on a wide variety of surfaces: sometimes on wallpaper, on which there was already a striped pattern, or some other design. On his expeditions – he used to go out two or three times a week – he would carry a small army knapsack, ochre in colour, inside which he would place whatever he needed to draw with. But he also used the knapsack to transport the things he found on his travels back to the house – things that he thought he might find a use for in future paintings, drawings or sculptures.

I remember once Joash telling me that he was painting on top of an old John Bratby painting; a used canvas that the artist had given him when he was at the Royal College.

Not only did Joash use a multitude of supports for his paintings but he also painted and made drawings on the inside pages of old books that he had bought. Usually these books contained black and white illustrations of the Modern School of Art or illustrations of old machinery or monuments. Some of the drawing were directly made over the printed texts and in others he transformed the etchings or the photographic plates into original works.

Though increasingly reclusive, he often went out to draw in the local allotment, bordering on Gledhow Valley Road, just opposite where we lived. He would also go on occasional trips outside of Leeds, if there was a festival or some colourful outdoor event, that included music and dancing. He certainly visited York on more than one occasion and I seem to remember him saying that he made some drawings of African dancers.

During the period before my leaving England, Joash did many paintings of my friends; including Peter Doefler, Danny Padmore, the writer, and Gilbert, the French exchange student, as well as portraits of my future wife Judith Allin.

In 1967 I got married and left for Canada. I visited Joash very occasionally on my visits to England from then until several years ago. It was during these visits that Joash also made drawings of our children Jason and Anna.

His work

Looking back now at Joash's work I am quite drawn to the still life paintings and drawings and very much the landscapes. Having also been a painter for a short time I have grown to understand how painters feel about their works. Not that they all feel the same – it depends on stylistic preference and values associated with differing styles.

What I value in Joash's paintings is, to coin a well used phrase, their 'painterliness'. That is – how the material surface feels. In paintings which are overtly about how things look, that is in a natural sense, the focus is often on the image, whether it can be considered one of verisimilitude or resemblance. In the case of Joash's painting the landscapes and the still lives are much more about traces, about the *signs* that the artist has left during the process of construction. So when we look at the paintings we can also experience its history. Nothing appears to be hidden. It's all on the surface. It is evident.

Often with paintings that are naturalistic and that use devices such as perspective the viewer is always at a distance. With Joash's painting we are always close to that surface, to that skin of paint. We can relive the motion and direction of the brush marks, the excitement of the accident, the spontaneity of the mark making. We can also sense the lack of inhibition, the almost unconscious childlike forces that we once as children knew so well.

What is also evident to me is the richness and subtly of the colour. After dispensing with the period of blue/blue-grey paintings Joash introduced colours in his paintings which were more personal, often having a range which is much warmer than the earlier colours. Rich browns and warm blues are often contrasted against leaf greens and turquoise blues. What I also find attractive about Joash's paintings is a quality that is hard to describe. I am reluctant to use words like primitive as I am aware of its perjorative sense and also I think that Joash's work is very sophisticated, often poetic and intensely personal. The word that I am seeking has to do with boldness – work that is both audacious and daunting and often humorous.

Perhaps what I mostly respond to is the element of *surprise* that I find in some of the work. We can never escape our own history. The period in which we live especially influences the way in which we view the world and this also applies to the modes of expression. Living in post-war England, being in London, seeing the works of the 'School of Paris', the 'Kitchen Sink' school: (Bratby, Jack Smith and all the rest) and also the work of painters like Kossoff, it is difficult to escape from immediate influences. So when I talk about *surprise*, it is the surprise of discovering in Joash's work an individual voice; paintings that remind the viewer of many works of his contemporaries, yet each possessing its own distinct qualities: a personal view that is rich, humorous and inventive.

Fig. 46 **Figure Study**
assemblage of found objects

Fig. 47 Drawings from 'The Magazine of Art', *circa* 1974

Portraits

Young Man Wearing Spectacles
Oil on sailcloth   61 × 46cm
Private collection

Portrait of Man on a Green Background
Oil on canvas   78 × 71cm

Portrait of Gilbert
Oil on sackcloth 71 × 61cm
Private collection

Gilbert Looking Down
Oil on sackcloth   72 × 61cm
Private collection

Portrait of a Man with Moustache
Oil on sackcloth 60 × 45.5cm
Private collection

Portrait of a Young Man
Oil on canvas   61 × 51cm

Man with a Moustache, Wearing a Green Jacket
Oil on sackcloth   89 × 59cm

Portrait of a Man
Oil on board 40.7 × 30.5cm
Private collection

Portrait of a Man with Large Ears
Oil on sackcloth 92 × 70cm

Portrait of a Man with a Beard
Oil on sackcloth 93 × 68cm
Private collection

Portrait of a Man
Oil on sackcloth 109 × 67cm

Peter Doefler I
Oil on hessian 92 ×83cm

Peter Doefler II
Oil on hessian 92 × 71cm

Peter Doefler III
Oil on sackcloth   92 × 71cm

Peter Doefler IV
Oil on sackcloth. Signed   104 × 67.5cm
Private collection

Girl Wearing a White Hat I
Oil on sackcloth   89.3 × 71cm

Girl Wearing a White Hat II
Oil on Canvas   106.5 × 71cm
Private collection

Portrait of a Girl with Blue and Pink Face
Oil on sackcloth 108 × 78cm

Portrait of a Seated Man Wearing Glasses
Oil on sackcloth   198 × 83cm

Portrait of a Man Wearing Glasses
Oil on sackcloth   90 × 70cm

Portrait of a Young Rabii
Oil on sackcloth 110 × 67.6cm

Portrait of a Young Woman Smiling
Oil on sackcloth   109 × 95cm
Private collection

Portrait of a Woman
Oil on sailcloth 77.5 × 66cm
Private collection

Young Woman in Blue and White
Oil on sackcloth 90 × 75cm
Private collection

Portrait of a Woman in a Red and Blue Striped Top
Oil on sackcloth   108 × 142cm

Woman in Pink and Blue
Oil on sackcloth   141.5 × 91.8cm
Private collection

Woman with a Striped Neck
Oil on sackcloth   107 × 74cm
Private collection

Woman Reading, I
Oil on sackcloth 123 × 92cm

Woman Reading, II
Oil on canvas 92 × 82cm

66

Woman with a Blue and Pink Face
Oil on canvas 86 × 76cm

Woman in a Red Hat
Oil on sackcloth   91 × 70cm
Private collection

Man with Yellow Lips
Oil on sackcloth   103 × 60cm

Portrait of a Man, I
Oil on hessian 92 × 82cm

Portrait of a Man, II
Oil on hessian   102 × 91cm

Young Woman Wearing a Red Striped Dress, I
Oil on sackcloth   203 × 109cm
Private collection

Young Woman Wearing a Striped Dress, II
Oil on sackcloth   194 × 109cm

Young Woman Wearing a Striped Dress, III
Oil on sackcloth   193 × 109cm

Portrait of a Man
Oil on sackcloth   108 × 83.5cm

Angry Figure in Blue and Red
Oil on sackcloth 108 x 83.5cm

Group studies

Two Gladiators
Oil on canvas   signed and dated
122 × 91cm

Knight and a Gladiator
Oil on canvas   signed and dated
147 × 119cm

Gladiators I
Oil on canvas   35 × 30cm

Gladiators II
Oil on canvas   31.5 × 42cm

Two Figures in a Garden I
Oil on board   123 × 145cm

Garden Landscape with Two Figures and a Long Billed Bird
Oil on board   213 × 160cm
Private collection

Two Figures in a Garden II
Oil on canvas 101 × 128cm

Woman and Child in a Garden
Oil on board 213 × 160cm
Private collection

Artist Painting in a Garden
Oil on board   213 × 160cm

Artist and Model in a Garden
Oil on board   160 × 161cm

Three Figures
Oil on sackcloth 110 × 122cm

Seated Figure Reading to His Companion
Oil on board   213 × 160cm

Seated Figures, One Reading to the Other
Oil on sackcloth   123 × 108cm

Two Seated Women
Oil on canvas 120 × 107cm

Two White Figures in a Dark Landscape
Oil on board   215 × 163cm

Scholar
Oil on sackcloth 123 × 91cm

Seated Figure with Symbolic Head
Oil on canvas   182.5 × 120.7cm

Circus Acrobats, I
Oil on board   77 × 99cm

The Athlete
Oil on board   70 × 77cm

Circus Acrobats II
Oil on advertising board   48 × 72cm

Fallen Dancer
Oil on board   56 × 38cm
Private collection

Seated Woman with Small Bearded Man
Oil on sackcloth 89 × 84cm
Private collection

Two Young Women
Oil on sackcloth 127.5 × 108cm

Young Girl on a Yellow Bicycle
Oil on sackcloth   130.5 × 112.5cm

Four Figures in Historical Costume
Oil on board 66 × 76cm
Private collection

Card Players
Oil on board 71 × 80cm

Three Figures Resting in a Landscape
Oil on board 69.5 × 76cm

The Artist and His Model
Oil board 66 × 76cm

The Picnic
Oil on board 70 × 76.5cm

99

White Figure Walking in a Dark Landscape
Oil on board   162 × 145cm

Two Figures in a Dark Landscape
Oil on board   144 × 123cm

Abstracted Figure in a Dark Landscape
Oil on board   215 × 163cm

Two White Figures in a Dark Landscape
Oil on board   122 × 91cm

Two Abstracted Figures in a Dark Landscape
Oil on board 160 × 145cm

Surrealist Landscape with Figures and Floating Chair
Oil on board   213 × 165cm

'The Professor of Metaphysics'
Oil on board   215 × 163cm
Submitted to the John Moores Exhibition in 1972
Private collection

Man and Woman Seated
Oil on board 213 × 160cm
Private collection

Seated Woman with Child in a Dark Landscape
Oil on board 213 × 160cm

Blue Monster
Oil on board 215 × 163cm

White Monster
Oil on board 213 × 160cm

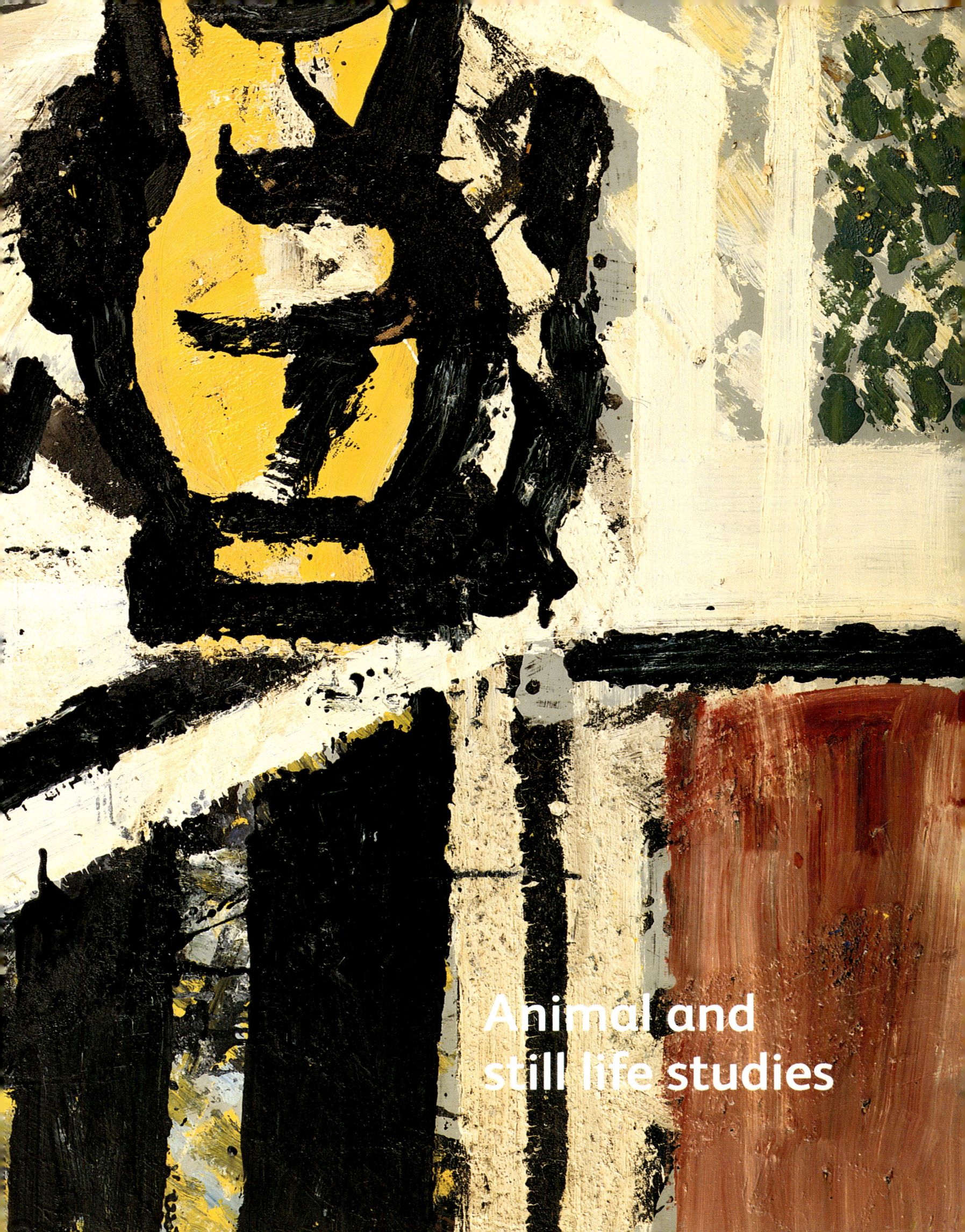

Animal and still life studies

Three Black Birds
Oil on sackcloth 145 × 122cm

'He Fights for Freedom and the Free World'
Signed and dated '65
Oil on sackcloth 120 × 100cm
Submitted the Cartwright Hall Summer Exhibition 1965
Private collection

White Cat in a Landscape
Oil on board 76.5 × 98.5cm

Bird with Yellow Beak in a Tree
Oil on board 77 × 121cm

Bird Table
Oil and straw on board 73 × 61cm

White Goat in a Landscape
Oil on board 151 × 121cm
Private collection

Black Goat
Oil on sackcloth   86.5 × 74.3cm
Private collection

White Goat
Oil on sackcloth 74 × 87cm
Private collection

Black and White Flowers
Oil on board 122 × 123cm

Irises
Oil on sackcloth 86 × 56.5cm
Private collection

Striped Jug and Bowl
Oil on sackcloth   117 × 100cm

Yellow Vase and Blue Vase with Flowers
Oil on sackcloth   77 × 61cm

Still Life on Yellow and Black
Oil on Board 76 × 65.5cm

Fragmented Table Top Still Life
Oil on board 122 × 183cm

Still Life with Bowl of Fruit and Cake
Oil and unbound pigment on sackcloth   112 × 96cm
Private collection

Still Life with Yellow Bowl
Oil on board   91.5 × 91cm

Blue Jug and Bowl of Yellow Fruit
Oil on hessian   70.7 × 91.8cm
Private collection

Crystal Clear – Crystal Fresh
Oil on advertising board   98 × 73.6cm
Private collection

Still Life with Jugs and Cup
Oil on board 76.5 × 99cm

White Jug and Vase of Flowers
Oil on board 92 × 91cm

Abstracted Still Life Forms
Oil on board   160 × 200cm

Still Life with Cup, Saucer and Coffee Pot
Oil on board 60 × 76cm

Vase of Flowers and a Jug
Oil on board 73 × 50.5cm

Still Life with Jug and Two Flowers
Oil on printed board 35 × 45cm

Still Life of Vases and Flowers on a Red Table Top
Oil on advertising board 61 × 58cm

Still Life with Four Blue Flowers
Oil on board 61 × 44 .5cm

Red Petals
Oil on canvas   63 × 45cm

White Jug with Red Flowers
Oil on board   31.8 × 21.5cm
Private collection

Cornflowers in a Blue and White Striped Vase
Oil on board 76 × 61cm
Private collection

Still Life of Seven Marguerites
Oil on board   86.3 × 68.8cm
Private collection

Daisies, Whisky Bottle & Tankard
Oil on board   76.8 × 59cm
Private collection

Still Life of Marguerites with Figurine
Oil on sackcloth 96.3 × 79cm

Still Life with Flowers
Oil on sackcloth 116 × 90cm
Private collection

Still Life of Cornflowers
Oil on board 60 × 70cm
Private collection

Still Life with Jug, Fish and Flowers
Oil on board   122 × 91cm
Private collection

Vase of Lilies
Oil on board 61.5 × 50cm
Private collection

Three Lilies
Oil on board 61 × 60.8cm

Lilies in a Blue and White Striped Vase
Oil on board 61 × 74cm
Private collection

Glass of Red Wine and a Jug, on a Silver Background
Oil on board   45.6 × 41.4cm

Glass of Red Wine and a Jug, on a Gold Background
Oil on board 45.9 × 41.5cm

Landscapes

Five Black Trees with Buildings Beyond
Oil on board 92 × 91cm

Pink Chimney
Oil on board 122 × 92cm

White Buildings
Oil on board 48 × 61cm

Landscape with Pink Pillared Building
Oil on board 135 × 122.2 cm
Private collection

Village Road
Oil and dry pigment on board 91 × 91cm
Private collection

Pink and Black Striped Roof
Oil on board 100 × 76cm

White Buildings with Black Chimney
Oil on board 75 × 99cm

Summer Landscape with White Building
Oil on board 91 × 81.5cm

Red and White Buildings Surrounded by Trees
Oil on board 193 cm × 159cm

Blue Sky and Clouds through Trees
Oil on board 122 × 184cm

Yellow Fence and Trees
Oil on board 215 × 165cm

Yellow Fence and Black Trees
Oil on board 122 × 121cm

Allotment Scene with Derelict Buildings
Oil on board 160 × 213cm

Row of Allotment Buildings
Oil on board 123 × 151cm

Abstracted Evening Landscape with Star
Oil on board. Signed
146 × 123cm

Abstracted Night Landscape
Oil on board 151 × 121cm

Woodland with Striped Trees
Oil on board   122 × 153cm

Urban Landscape with Large Trees
Oil on board   101 × 122cm

White Allotment Building
Oil on board 122 × 145cm

Allotments with White Building
Oil on board 123 × 161cm

Allotment Buildings with Trees in the Foreground
Oil on board 100 × 121.5cm

Allotments with Two Trees
Oil on board 124 × 145cm

Four Trees
Oil on board 160 × 130cm

Telegraph Pole, Trees and Industrial Buildings
Oil on board 121 × 151cm

Single Tree with White Fence
Oil on board 92 × 80.5cm

Birds on a Wire
Oil on board 145 × 122cm

White Picket Fence with Trees and Buildings Beyond
Oil on board 123 × 123cm

Fenced Pathway through Allotments
Oil on board 122 × 122cm

White Picket Fences
Oil on board. Signed
125 × 124cm

Allotment Scene with Single White Cloud
Oil on board 92 × 114cm

Allotments, Fences and Watertower
Oil on board   121 × 121cm

Cityscape with Two White Clouds
Oil on board   100 × 122cm

Industrial Landscape – Leeds
Oil on board 110 × 128.5cm

Path with White Fence
Oil on board 92 × 91cm

The White Shed
Oil on board 92 × 91cm

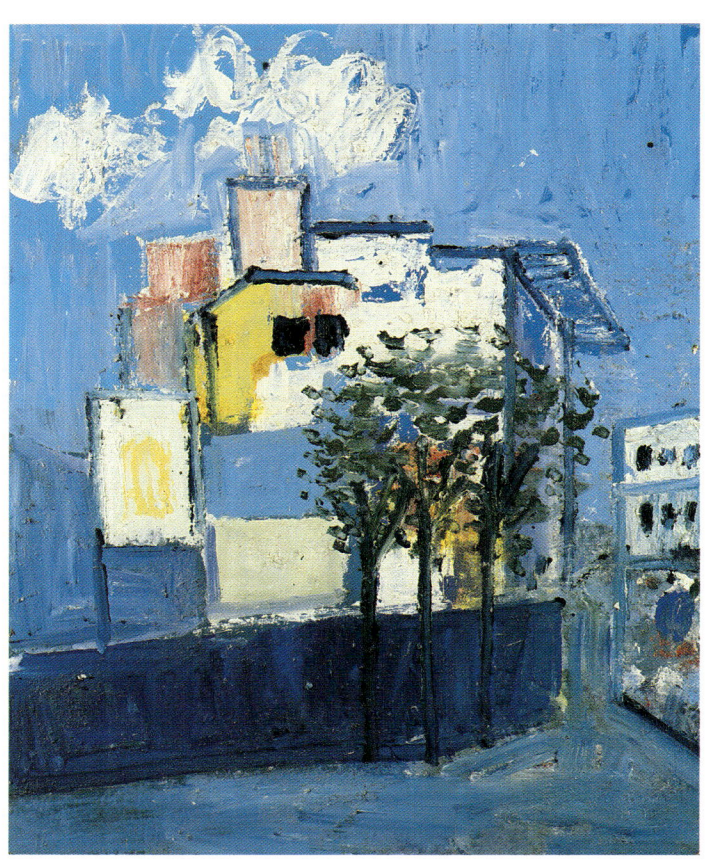

Bright City Buildings
Oil on board   122 × 100cm

Tall City Buildings with Trees in the Foreground
Oil on board   160 × 145cm

Coloured Hoardings with Trees and High Rise City Buildings
Oil on board   93 × 122cm

Cityscape with Two Trees in the Foreground
Oil on board   107 × 91cm

Black Fence, Trees and Buildings
Oil on board   76 × 99cm

Landscape with Orange Dot
O l on board   90 × 80cm

Cityscape with Trees in the Foreground
Oil on board 122 × 100cm

Landscape with Yellow Trees
Oil on board 122 × 122cm

Allotments
Oil on board 73 × 61.2cm

Urban Landscape
Oil on board 84 × 99cm

Allotments
Oil on board 92 × 91cm

Trees and Outbuildings
Oil on board   145 × 122cm

Allotments
Oil on board 92 × 91cm

Lilac Fence with Overgrown Allotments
Oil on board 122 × 145cm

Drawings, collage and sculpture

Leeds City Development
Gouache 48 × 60cm

Victorian Buildings, Leeds
Pencil on paper 38 × 54cm

Boats and Bridge, Leeds
Pencil drawing 38 × 54cm

Waterway, Leeds Centre
Pencil drawing   38 × 54cm

Boat Masts
Pencil drawing 38 × 54cm

Whitby Harbour
Pencil on paper 35 × 43cm

Lighthouse Viewed Through Trees
Graphite and coloured pencil on paper
35 × 43cm

North East Fishing Village
Graphite and coloured pencil on paper
Signed and dated 28–8–79
61 × 71cm

Landscape with Corn Crops
Pencil on paper   35 × 45cm
Private collection

Harvested Crops with Two Clouds
Pencil on paper   35 × 45cm
Private collection

Rural Landscape
Graphite and coloured pencil on paper
35 × 45cm
Private collection

Landscape with Outbuildings
Graphite and coloured pencil on paper
35 × 45cm
Private collection

Garden with Obscured Building
Pencil on paper   46 × 52cm
Private collection

Country Lane with Stone Wall
Pencil on paper 36 × 44.5cm
Private collection

Portrait of a Man and Woman
Pastel and chalk on paper   51 × 64cm

Man with a Cigarette and Two Other Figures
Pastel and chalk on paper 51 × 64cm

Birds in Foliage
Pastel and chalk on paper
51 × 64cm

Bearded Man on a White Horse with a Standing Figure
Pastel and chalk on paper   64 × 51cm
Private collection

Allotment Building
Watercolour 35 × 43cm
Private collection

Yellow Landscape with Telegraph Pole
Watercolour 35 × 43cm
Private collection

Still Life with Fish and Jug of Flowers
Collage 45 × 60cm
Private collection

Two Vases
Collage 60 × 60cm
Private collection

No. 41
Collage 55 × 38cm
Private collection

No. 41
Collage 55 × 38cm
Private collection

Six Marguerites in an Oriental Vase
Collage and chalk on paper 78 × 52cm
Private collection

Plant Study
Black ink on paper   78 × 52cm
Private collection

Study for 'Surrealist Landscape with Figures and Floating Chair' (see page 104)
Pen and ink on paper 77 × 52cm
Private collection

Monster
Pen and ink on paper   77 × 52cm
Private collection

Portrait of a Man Wearing a Hat
Pencil on paper 78 × 52cm
Private collection

Portrait of a Young Woman Wearing a Headband
Pencil on paper   78 × 52cm
Private collection

Portrait of a Young Rabbi
Charcoal on paper   78 × 52cm
Private collection

Young Woman with Long Hair
Pencil on paper 78 × 52cm
Private collection

Portrait of a Woman with Blue Face and Red Lips
Charcoal and chalk on paper   64 × 51.5cm

Woman with a Ruff and Striped Dress
Oil on wallpaper 91 × 53.5cm

Head
Oil paint on motor bicycle tank 42 × 32cm

Figure Study
Assemblage of found objects 76 × 31cm

Composition
Assemblage of found objects   91.5 × 398cm

The Books

The following images have been taken from the eight leather bound and linen covered 'Magazine's of Art' mentioned earlier in this book. Published in the late nineteenth century Joash used the illustrations and text within the books to provide a background for his own compositions. Full of sketches, drawings and collage the books include many finished drawings for his large scale paintings including *The Professor of Metaphysics* (see page 105) and *Seated Woman with Child* (see page 107).

Collectors

Mrs J Anthony	Andrew & Michele Martin
Mr & Mrs Bebbington	Mr & Mrs Ian Moore
Mr & Mrs R Bentley	P.J. Moore
Clare Berry	Simon Morris
Howard Bilton	Patricia Mounter
The Blake Collection	Mr Bob Norton
Nick Bradford	Greg O'Shea
Mr Bucking	J.P.
Dr & Mrs Butt	Dr & Mrs C & S Pease
Mr & Mrs L.A. Charneca	Greg Renton
Mrs Elizabeth Clarke	Jonathan Rosenhead
Dr Paul Clarke	Dr Ian Ross
Emma Abby Collins	Elizabeth Rowe
Robbie Cowan	Mr & Mrs D Simpson
Daphne Cotton	Mrs Lilian Slowe
Mark Davis	Mr & Mrs A. Smith
Peter & Jackie Davis	Peter A. Smith
Sam Dawson	Mr & Mrs Steven Smith
Simon Dawson	Mr R Wade Smith
Peter Doefler	Jonathan Sparey
Christopher Donald	Susan Spencer
Mr & Mrs Hugh Dunn	Mr & Mrs Spooner
Mr & Mrs Martin Ephson	Professor Hugo Mascie Taylor
Gillian Eynor	Paul Thomas
Gillian Freedman	Frances Thorn
Mrs Gilliard	Mr & Mrs John Thorp
David Goodfellow	Selina Thorp
Peter Goodwin	Graham Walsh
J Gowland	Sue Warrior
Anthony Graham	Trevor Weiner
Unity Heald	I.G.W. White
Neil Holroyd	Mr & Mrs J Wilks
Stephen Hoyle	Mrs Williams
R Jenkins	Mr & Mrs Trevor Wilson
Maxine Kidd	Yvonne Wilson
Mr & Mrs Graham Leigh	Graeme & Sharon Wood
Paul Longstaff	Tim Wood
Mr & Mrs Lovelady	Mr & Mrs Wynn